NEWPORT SHINGLE STYLE

NEWPORT SHINGLE STYLE

Cheryl Hackett

Photography by Kindra Clineff

F

FRANCES LINCOLN LIMITED
PUBLISHERS

CONTENTS

FOREWORD
Written by Richard Guy Wilson   6

INTRODUCTION
Written by Cheryl Hackett   10

AMERICAN COLONIAL HERITAGE
1. Whitehall   20

STICK STYLE
2. Chalet Stables   24

QUEEN ANNE STYLE
3. William Watts Sherman House 30

NINETEENTH CENTURY
4. Samuel Tilton House   36
5. Isaac Bell House   42
6. Channel Bells   48

TWENTIETH CENTURY
7. Wildacre   56
8. Seabright   64
9. Highland House   70

TWENTY-FIRST CENTURY
10. Blackwatch   76
11. Out to Sea   82
12. Beavertail House   88
13. Eastwell House   94
14. Sulthorne   100
15. Bancroft on the Bluffs   106

Bibliography   110
Index   110
Acknowledgements   111
Contributors   111

FOREWORD

WRITTEN BY
RICHARD GUY WILSON

The Isaac Bell House introduced me to the Shingle Style. During the mid-1960s while a young naval officer in Newport, Rhode Island, practically every day I turned the corner at Bellevue Avenue and Perry Street where the huge asymmetrical shingled mass and the wonderful porch posts caught my eye. Finally I stopped and asked if I could look inside since then it was a home for the elderly. The great hall, fireplace, flowing stairs, wide doorways and the way the interior opened to the porch amazed me. I then discovered other Newport buildings – not so much the giant mansions such as the Breakers and Rosecliff (though I have come to like them) – but the Casino, the William Watts Sherman House and on back streets some obscure shingled houses that fellow officers lived in such as the Samuel Tilton House. Finally, I went to the library – then located in Richard Upjohn's Edward King Villa – and discovered Antoinette Downing and Vincent Scully's *The Architectural Heritage of Newport, Rhode Island* (1952) and Scully's classic, *The Shingle Style* (1955). Not too long thereafter I left the Navy, went to graduate school, wrote some papers for an architectural history course, and ultimately did my Ph.D. dissertation (and later a book) on the architecture of McKim, Mead & White, who designed the Isaac Bell House, Samuel Tilton House, and Rosecliff, along with the Newport Casino, and assisted on the William Watts Sherman House. Turning a corner can change one's life.

Scully's *The Shingle Style* argued that in the 1870s and 1880s a few American architects invented a new architecture which helped foster twentieth century modernism. The book was a reaction to the almost exclusive focus of architects and historians upon the European origins of Modernism but as Scully's subtitle *Architectural Theory and Design from Richardson to the Origins of Wright* indicated, there were American origins as well, particularly in the open plan. Since Scully's path-breaking book, numerous scholars and writers have enlarged upon the Shingle Style, showing different permeations and how it influenced many others such as the California Arts and Crafts architects Greene & Greene, and Irving Gill, who designed several houses in Newport.

The original architects would have been puzzled by the term 'Shingle Style' since it was an invention of the 1950s. Back in the later nineteenth century they would have used the terms 'Queen Anne', 'Modernized Colonial' and 'Resort Style'. But Shingle Style has caught on and entered into the American vocabulary as a style of the period.

The various terms originally used give a clue to some of the origins of the Shingle Style and its importance in Newport. Newport, to put it simply, was for a period of 15–20 years, the center of American design. The architects were very influenced by their contemporaries in England who were

BELOW LEFT The Isaac Bell House. McKim, Mead & White's liberal use of shingles quickly became one the architectural firm's trademarks.

BELOW The William Watts Sherman House has a massive gable and horizontal elements which signify the emergence of Shingle Style.

searching for an English idiom and came up with the Queen Anne and the Olde English styles. These styles travelled across the Atlantic in various magazines and illustrations and were picked up by a younger generation of American architects such as H.H. Richardson, Charles McKim, Stanford White, Bruce Price, Clarence Luce, Charles Bevins and others. But they didn't just copy the English, they made changes relying on the American penchant for wood. Instead of hung clay tiles or slate that the English used, Americans turned back to wooden shingles that had been employed in the Colonial period. The Americans, inspired by the English rummaging through their past for details, turned to American Colonial features such as large long sloping roofs, double gables, fan lights over doors, and small classical details. Also inspiring the Americans was Japanese architecture (Commodore M. Perry, a Newporter, opened Japan to the

West in 1853), as can been seen in the turned bamboo porch posts of the Isaac Bell House or the piazza at the Newport Casino. The interiors also differed from English models with large halls and flowing staircases and the ground floor rooms opened into each other and to the porch or piazza. The houses contained an organic element and as the shingles weathered they seemed to grow from their site.

Although the Shingle Style appeared in numerous locations along the East Coast back in the 1870s and then spread inland and ultimately to the West Coast, Newport acted as the center and in a sense the catalyst. The tremendous amount of seventeenth- and eighteenth-century architecture inspired the architects and Charles McKim in particular conducted research and published a limited edition book of plates entitled 'Old Newport Houses.' In a brief article he argued that the weathered shingled roof of an eighteenth-century house was the true source for an American architecture.

By the mid-1960s a small Shingle Style revival was underway. The original Shingle style appealed with its sense of informality, spirit of summer, and the rugged

quality that recalled the past, but not in a strict sense. Scully participated in this revival with his book of 1974, *The Shingle Style Today, or the Historian's Revenge*. An element of this revival lay with the advent of Post-Modernism which was opposed to the starkness and machine type elements of some modernist houses. Instead of smooth mirror-like finishes and abstract elements such as flat roofs houses should have texture, warmth, and pitched roofs.

Cheryl Hackett is the first person to treat this new Shingle Style while paying attention to its historic roots in Newport. As a Newporter she knows both the original houses and their origins in early Newport and the new ones created by Bernard Wharton, William Burgin, John Grosvenor, Paul Weber and Paul Burke. To call these new houses simply a revival is inaccurate; their architects build upon the foundations set down over a century ago. In form and shingles they recall the past but alternatively the new houses contain modern spaces, comforts, views, and materials. They demonstrate the continuing relevance of the style and that maybe some time in the future a person passing in front of them will have his or her life changed.

OPPOSITE Green Animals
Topiary Gardens.

LEFT Ochre Court.

INTRODUCTION

WRITTEN BY
CHERYL HACKETT

Newport, Rhode Island, is an idyllic isle where a sumptuous variety of seascapes, seafaring history, and stunning architecture rein supreme. A myriad of Colonial, Federal, Greek Revival and Victorian structures lovingly preserved as homes or thoughtfully repurposed as inns, galleries, boutiques, eateries and offices define the City-by-the-Sea and enchant residents and visitors alike with vestiges of the past.

Newport was a thriving seaport in the seventeenth and eighteenth centuries. After the Civil War, prosperity redefined the coastal hamlet and Newport experienced a building boom of epic proportions. Architects from the nation's most venerable firms descended upon the city armed with their wealthy clients' visions for summer 'cottages' that resembled European chateaux and villas. While colossal mansions were being built along Bellevue Avenue, the Cliff Walk and Ocean Drive, intellectuals and artists from Boston and Philadelphia were commissioning impressive residences just a few blocks away from 'Millionaires' Row'. Noted architects turned Newport into an architectural laboratory where many styles were tested and perfected. And like a symphony, countless carpenters and tradesmen from around the world filled the air with the distinct rhythm of sawing and hammering and the melody of progress.

The Shingle Style, considered an American original architectural achievement, flourished in Newport and its Gilded Age environs during the 1880s. Unlike many nineteenth-century symmetrical homes constructed mostly of brick, Shingle Style structures featured asymmetrical wood frames and shingled stories set dramatically on stone foundations. These romantic homes were intended to blend with the surrounding landscape, so the wave, diamond and saw tooth patterned shingles were left to weather naturally. Shingle Style exteriors incorporated decidedly Colonial, Stick Style and Queen Anne elements such as gables, gambrel roofs, brick and stone chimneys, bands of small-paned windows, turrets, columns

and pediments. And the interiors contained imaginative staircases, art glass windows, hand-crafted millwork and emphasized organized space and open floor plans for gracious living. Most importantly, nearly every room boasted large and freely spaced windows and doors that opened to porches strategically positioned to take full advantage of ocean views and cool summer breezes. Most fittingly, noted architectural critic Vincent Scully would later hail these early Shingle Style homes as 'the Architecture of the American summer'.

Wonderfully preserved nineteenth-century Shingle Style homes still distinguish Newport's legendary historic districts and serve as muses to new generations of architects, interior designers, builders and homeowners who share a collective passion for this unique vernacular that holds a deep reverence for history, follows form and function and boasts an organic aesthetic. Recently, American architecture has witnessed a renaissance as impressive new Shingle Style homes are built alongside those that have presided along the rugged Rhode Island coastline for more than a century. Attention to detail is so exquisite that the latest interpretations are often mistaken for nineteenth-century originals causing casual observers to ponder – is that Shingle Style, then or now?

The collection of homes showcased in this book have the same spirit running through them and their designs work in tandem to embody architectural critic Vincent Scully's sentiment towards Shingle Style: 'The variety was like that of a nineteenth-century landscape painting, where graduations of light – partly in full flood, partly shielded by porches; sometimes golden, sometimes thunderous – defined flickering interior landscapes at various levels, broader and more extensive than any that Americans had known before and flowing on to the outside through wide doors and echoing porches.'

LEFT International Tennis Hall of Fame.

BELOW Bowens Wharf.

RIGHT Marble House.

AMERICAN
COLONIAL
HERITAGE

CHAPTER 1

WHITEHALL

OPPOSITE Eighteenth-century scholars gathered at Whitehall to discuss philosophy with Anglican cleric, educator and philosopher, Bishop Berkeley, while he resided there between 1729 and 1731. Berkeley wrote *Alciphron or the Minute Philosopher* while living at Whitehall.

LEFT Named for the palace of English Kings from Henry VIII to James II, Whitehall is one of the first vernacular buildings in the United States to feature Palladian details such as the formal façade, pedimented false double front door and modillion cornice of flat blocks.

When architects scanned the pages of the *New York Sketchbook of Architecture* in January 1874, the first published photograph of an American home held their gaze. The momentous image did not feature the symmetrical Georgian façade of Bishop George Berkeley's house built amongst bucolic farmlands in Middletown, Rhode Island, in 1728–9. Instead the camera captured the less formal long sloping gable that distinguished the hipped roof's lean-to construction. Historians credit Charles Follen McKim as being responsible for publishing the photograph. The rising young architect, who would later establish McKim, Mead & White, the largest and most celebrated nineteenth-century architectural firm, looked to seventeenth- and eighteenth-century structures for inspiration. The image along with subsequent images, renderings and articles advocating the Colonial period stirred curiosity for domestic architecture built around the same time our forefathers framed the Constitution.

Two years after the photograph caused a sensation, the United States celebrated their centennial. Amid the parade of broad stripes and bright stars, the nation reflected on a century of brave history and developed a deeper sense of national pride and appreciation for their Colonial heritage. Suddenly, 'American' and 'New World' became fashionable terms. A collection of Colonial homes at the 1876 Centennial Exposition in Philadelphia heightened architects' appreciation for New World designs. The following year, McKim and his friends Stanford White, William Mead and William Bigelow embarked on a sketching tour of Colonial structures and remains situated along the New England coast. The architects visited Cape Cod, Nantucket and the North Shore of Boston and noted the spatial, structural and textural designs of early settlers' homes sheathed in wooden shingles. In the ensuing years, the most prolific architects set out to create a new breed of architecture that echoed America's ancestral past through Colonial-style architectural elements.

STICK STYLE

CHAPTER 2
CHALET STABLES

OPPOSITE A replication of the original Chalet Stable was designed as a companion piece to the enlarged stable block. The new edifice built in 2006 houses a garage, pool and studio.

RIGHT The exterior modifications removed a 1907 addition at the northeast corner that restores the symmetry of the east facing gable. Chamfered Stick Style framing of the original porte-cochere was recreated on the north elevation under the center gable applied to the siding. Two doors under the gable were modified with shed roof covers. Small windows on the first floor reflected the stable windows framed in the wall at some previous time.

Stick Style also influenced the development of Shingle Style. Vincent Scully coined the term in the mid-twentieth century to describe domestic architecture that emphasized interior structure through exterior detailing consisting of vertical, horizontal and diagonal members that skeletontized the exterior. Newport's status as a summer colony was gaining momentum at the time and many villas and cottages were being constructed with highly ornamental facades featuring vertical board and battens with decorative cut-outs, diagonal bracing and gables with brackets and exposed trusses. The interplay of light and shadow emphasized the geometric elements and made the houses seem even more picturesque.

Richard Morris Hunt designed several Stick Style and similar Chalet Style homes in Newport during the later part of the nineteenth century. Hunt, hailed as the 'Dean of American Architecture', was a leading figure of the Gilded Age and widely admired throughout the United States and Europe for his intelligence, enthusiasm, diplomacy, pride in his New England roots, and above all his refined aesthetic perceptions. He was the first American to attend the Ecole des Beaux Arts in Paris and the first American to receive a gold medal from the Royal Institute for British Architects. When designing buildings, Hunt often looked to the past for inspiration.

Hunt's most notable Stick Style design in Newport is the John N.A. Griswold House built in 1864. Although the Griswold House has garnered considerable attention among architectural historians, the Chalet Stables, a lesser known commission, has captured the spotlight in recent years. Mrs Coleford Jones commissioned Hunt in 1867 to design the Chalet Stables as a small carriage barn and stable to service and complement the main Chalet Estate built several years before, overlooking Newport Harbor. Like many old outbuildings on waterfront estates, the Chalet Stables have undergone three renovations and enlargements since its creation. Subsequently, the alterations disguised Hunt's unique style. The structure remained in obscurity until architect and homeowner John Grosvenor uncovered Hunt's original drawings at the Octagon House in Washington, D.C. The documents revealed the amazing degradation of Hunt's powerful Stick and Chalet Styles and massing. Grosvenor, a founding principal of Newport Collaborative Architects, Inc., has extensive experience in historic preservation and adaptive reuse and set out to replicate the building's original façade, create a new interior and build a new garage and pool house that closely resembled Hunt's original plan for the Chalet Stables.

ABOVE The new interiors captured an Arts and Crafts vernacular utilizing fir floors and doors with maple header rails and trim throughout the living and dining room areas.

RIGHT The remaining interior detail remnants included 150-year-old beaded board ceilings and the original post and beam construction of the stable's super structure.

OPPOSITE A two-sided fireplace and frieze of hand-painted murals serve as focal points in the dining room.

QUEEN ANNE STYLE

CHAPTER 3

WILLIAM WATTS SHERMAN HOUSE

The Queen Anne Style also influenced Shingle Style. In 1876, a new magazine that acted as a spokesman for a rising professional class of architects was founded. The early issues of the *American Architect and Building News* discussed Queen Anne influences at length and merited Olde English half-timbered designs with large living halls and bay windows.

Two years before architectural circles were advocating the Queen Anne style, Henry Hobson Richardson was exploring the style in Newport at the William Watts Sherman House built between 1874 and 1876. Richardson designed the summer 'cottage' near Bellevue Avenue for a wealthy New York banker. The decidedly vertical structure features an impressive central gable cut with a horizontal band of windows accented by an elaborate shingled upper story with undercut porches and balconies. The home's façade exhibits bold patterns and textures achieved through innovative combinations of wood carvings, rustic stone, brick masonry, jig-sawn shingles and half-timbering insets.

The interiors were designed by Stanford White when he was a young designer working in Richardson's office. The spatial qualities are distinguished by a central living hall with a hooded fireplace and a dramatic staircase crafted with multiple landings. White's perspective drawing of the William Watts Sherman House was published in an 1875 issue of the *New York Sketchbook of Architecture*, popularizing Richardson and further acquainting the public with an original American architectural form.

A tapestry of architectural elements is achieved by the combination of rough granite, stucco and timbers, and patterned shingles.

OPPOSITE A pair of brick masonry chimneys recall a romantic English aesthetic.

LEFT The prominent gable with an oriel window and a pair of porches playfully extends over the foundation.

BELOW In 1881, Stanford White transformed the drawing room in the William Watts Sherman House into a library resplendent with Colonial, Oriental and Arts and Crafts motifs, green paneling and gold-leaf embellishments.

NINETEENTH CENTURY

CHAPTER 4

SAMUEL TILTON HOUSE

McKim, Mead & White were masters of the Shingle Style. They were the largest and most recognized architectural firm of the Victorian period and completed more than a thousand commissions between 1879 and 1912. The Samuel Tilton House built in Newport in 1881 represents one of the firm's earliest Shingle Style compositions that reflect a relaxed aesthetic.

Situated in the heart of the Kay Street/ Catherine Street/ Old Beach Road historic district, the modest cottage's original nineteenth-century architectural features remain intact. Perhaps what makes this house so unique is the variety of ornamentation showcased on different elevations. For example, the street facing façade is characterized by rough cut granite, half timbers, an array of patterned shingles and stucco panels embellished with a shield and sunburst mosaic fashioned from pieces of colored glass, shells, pebbles and coal. The three-storey garden elevation is accentuated by bands of asymmetrical windows, and porches contained within a broad main gable.

The interior is organized around a central hall that allows living spaces to flow into each other. The elaborate textured ceilings, leaded glass windows, spindle screens, metal fixtures and woodwork draw inspiration from Japan, India and Great Britain.

PREVIOUS PAGE Samuel Tilton House staircase.

RIGHT The mass of the Samuel Tilton House is contained under one gable.

ABOVE The brick masonry
chimneys are similar to those
built throughout New England
during the seventeenth century.

RIGHT The northwest elevation
features a dynamic combination
of building materials including
stone, timbers and stucco.

The living room retains the
original green built-in seats
beside a fireplace with Colonial
shell motifs and gold accents.

ABOVE The central hall has fancy turned spindles and fireplace with pale orange marble.

LEFT The music room is grand in scale with vertical elements emphasized by three tall cottage windows.

CHAPTER 5

ISAAC BELL HOUSE

OPPOSITE With the help of early photographs and nineteenth-century tools, new shingles for the Isaac Bell House were cut and laid in wave and scale patterns in the 1990s.

LEFT Mrs Bell's bedroom is resplendent with a plaster basket weave frieze, elegant fireplace, built-in drawers with fancy hardware, and a window bay with multi-paned windows.

Considered the finest example of Shingle Style architecture in the United States, the Isaac Bell House is another masterful work designed by McKim, Mead & White. Isaac Bell was a member of an old New York family whose personal fortune came through inheritance and his success as a cotton broker. In 1877, at the age of 31, Bell retired and the following year he married Jeanette Bennett, the sister of newspaper magnate James Gordon Bennett. About the same time Bell was enjoying his honeymoon, his brother-in-law had commissioned the newly formed architectural firm of McKim, Mead & White to design the Newport Casino in the Shingle Style. The project was completed in 1881 and immediately became the hub of Newport's high society. Later that same year, Bell commissioned McKim, Mead & White to build his summer home on the corner of Bellevue Avenue and Perry Street.

What impressed architectural critics most about the Isaac Bell House was its innovative combination of historic features. Colonial America inspired the two sweeping gables and the sash windows. Medieval European towers inspired the curved shape of the two-storey veranda. The Far East inspired the piazza supported by columns carved to resemble bamboo. The piazza spans the entire east side of the house and meets a bell-shaped tower reminiscent of Colonial windmills.

Two important exterior features incorporated into the Isaac Bell House are the entrance and the patterned shingles. Many Victorian-era homes featured a grand entrance as the focal point of the exterior. The entrance to the house is placed off to the side of the building and is quite informal with porches opening to landscaped grounds. Whimsical carved wooden dolphin brackets support the entrance's roof. Cedar shingles were widely used in the 1870s, so to distinguish the house from other homes built during the same period, McKim, Mead & White utilized decorative shingles cut to resemble waves and diamonds. The interior of the Isaac Bell House emphasizes organized space with open floor plans. The unique inglenook with a fireplace and surrounding sitting area inspires relaxed and gracious living.

ABOVE McKim, Mead & White designed a perfect Shingle Style home that would influence future generations of architects, including Frank Lloyd Wright.

FAR LEFT During the Gilded Age, the public caught glimpses of the wealthy relaxing and socializing on the open porches and verandas.

LEFT The main gate at the Isaac Bell House.

OPPOSITE The formal dining room has textured ceilings and walls, leaded glass over mantel, and a built-in buffet.

RIGHT Windows of colored and bottle glass usher light into the stair hall.

BELOW RIGHT The main staircase seen through the carved screen.

CHAPTER 6

CHANNEL BELLS

Charles Lovatt Bevins was born in Manchester, England in 1844 and immigrated to New England in 1878. Bevins eventually moved to Rhode Island and designed more than forty significant resort homes in Jamestown, Rhode Island for wealthy and influential clients who summered on the scenic island. Bevins' English background and experience working at the Boston-based architectural firm of Peabody and Stearns led him to emphasize the Queen Anne style in his own Shingle Style interpretations. Although Bevins' designs still punctuate Jamestown's scenic coastline, he is virtually unknown among historians and architectural sources have yet to mention him.

Channel Bells, designed by Bevins in 1888 for General Robert Patterson, captures the English architect's penchant for vertical massing, selective ornamentation and generous porches that function as outdoor living rooms. Channel Bells presides on a bluff with panoramic views of Newport Harbour and Narragansett Bay. Bevins' signature style is defined by a gable, hip, gambrel and saltbox forms that rise in a pyramidal form. The main entrance is strategically positioned off to the side to allow a series of multi-paned windows, raised panels and stained glass to heighten the edifice's visual interest. Unlike other Shingle Style architects of the day who favoured wave, diamond and fish scale shaped shingles, Bevins preferred the simple un-cut variety to express the fluidity of a house's exterior.

As a contemporary to McKim, Mead & White, Bevins maintained an office in nearby Newport and most likely was influenced by the firm's work. Channel Bells' interior spaces recall Colonial detailing in the woodwork, fireplaces and textured ceilings. The rooms circulate around a central living hall with a dramatic corner fireplace and wide stair hall. Many of the rooms open to covered porches and the elegant flow encourages Bevins' architectural charms to unfold in a delightful sequence.

Bevins' interpretation of the early Shingle Style is evident in the vertical massing of the façade, further distinguished by a stunning combination of multi-paned windows, raised panels and stained glass.

ABOVE A band of windows maximizes water views from the second storey master bedroom.

FAR LEFT Small windows on the addition recalls nineteenth-century style and expands the water views from the kitchen.

LEFT The covered veranda looks towards Narragansett Bay and Newport in the distance.

BELOW An abundance
of windows adds to the
ambiance of the entry hall that
features elaborate woodwork
on the walls and ceilings and
a dramatic staircase.

A pair of corner fireplaces
in the entry hall and dining
room demonstrates form
and function.

LEFT A textured ceiling showcases Bevins' affinity for geometric embellishments.

BELOW The origins of the carved shells on the over mantel in the dining room can be traced to the Colonial era.

TWENTIETH CENTURY

CHAPTER 7
WILDACRE

Irving J. Gill is widely recognized as the first prominent architect of the Modernist era and one of California's most important architects. He designed hundreds of homes, schools, churches and institutional buildings in San Diego during the late nineteenth and early twentieth centuries and his prolific buildings ranged from half-timbered mansions with massive stone foundations to unornamented abstract designs that drew inspiration from Pueblo missions and traditions. Although his work defined West Coast architecture, his philosophy emanates in a Shingle Style home he designed in Newport in 1901 that quietly serves as a testimony to his ingenious style and technical ability.

Success broadened Gill's social circle and while at a dance at the Coronado Hotel in San Diego, he met Albert Olmsted, son of famed landscape architect Frederick Law Olmsted, Jr., who designed New York's Central Park. Olmsted persuaded Gill to build him a mansion on a seven-acre granite outcropping on Newport's legendary Ocean Avenue. For Wildacre, Gill created a home with flowing and dynamic spaces stretching upwards and outwards. The exterior features indigenous shingle work set on a cobblestone foundation. A variety of angular shapes, gabled dormers, gambrel and a cobblestone chimney work in tandem to echo the Shingle Style. And decidedly West Coast elements, including corner windows that drop into a parapet wall borrowed from the McKenzie House he designed in Coronado in 1898 and California redwood interiors, express Gill's unique artistry. Panoramic water views serve as the focal point of virtually every room in the home that has been completely restored by the current owner. Colonial-style features, such as arched brick fireplaces and coved ceilings underscore the home's elegance. Strategically positioned outlooks form a seamless connection with the surrounding landscape and the stunning Rhode Island seascape.

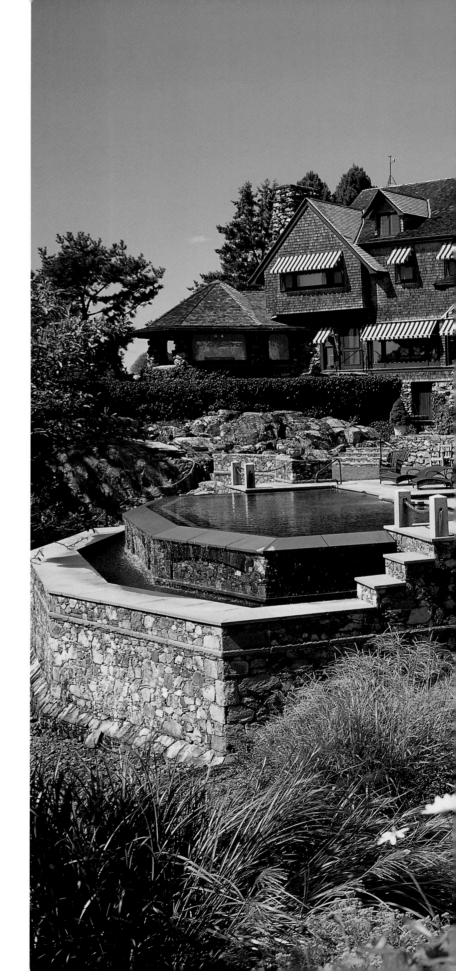

LEFT Wildacre, designed by Iriving Gill in 1901, presides on a granite outcropping overlooking Price's Neck. The house recently underwent a 10-year restoration.

ABOVE An eyebrow window lends a whimsical touch to the new pool house.

FAR LEFT The new infinity edge pool, pool house and stone walls are carefully integrated into the cliff and blend effortlessly with the home.

LEFT A stone urn contains a unique assortment of perennials.

Polished wood beams tie
seamlessly into rafters in
the study appointed with
an Oriental décor.

LEFT The main living spaces are organized around the central entry hall.

BELOW Finished beamed ceilings enhance the dining room's structural integrity.

CHAPTER 8

SEABRIGHT

A century after Shingle Style helped shape Newport's architectural heritage, architect William Burgin revisited the style to design a residence on Ocean Avenue in 1987. Seabright is a five-storey home built on a granite outcropping overlooking a salt marsh, Ocean Avenue, and the Atlantic Ocean. Seabright's dramatic diagonal sweeping gable, circular porch and brick and stone chimneys draw inspiration from nineteenth-century Shingle Style homes. Having been influenced early on by the work of McKim, Mead & White, Burgin, a principal at Burgin Lambert Architects, envisioned a Shingle Style home perched atop a rugged granite outcrop in the middle of dense ocean stunted scrub.

Burgin had produced variations on modernist resort homes for numerous residences, but his groundbreaking Shingle Style design was a welcome departure from the boxy contemporary building trends that had populated the venerable Ocean Avenue neighbourhood since the mid-twentieth century. A grand sloping roof, classic columns, stone and red brick chimneys, hipped dormers, screened porch with bedroom deck above and a rear stair tower all reflect the massing and details of early Shingle Style homes, particularly the Isaac Bell House.

Seabright's interior, however, is thoroughly modern and soars above the scrub and rocks to allow every room ample views of the ocean and inlet. The main living spaces are situated on the third storey. Expansive windows, French doors and a wraparound porch form a seamless connection between indoor and outdoor living spaces and provide a variety of views within the house. A cantilever staircase connects the formal living area with the more intimate bedrooms situated on the fourth and fifth floors. Recalling a ship's crow's nest, south facing windows in the master bedroom infuse the suite with light and provide unobstructed views of Rhode Island Sound and poignant glimpses of neighbouring architectural treasures such as Wildacre.

Seabright's stacked porches and stacked hipped dormers draw inspiration from the historic Isaac Bell House. The circular elements give depth to the narrowness of the house.

ABOVE The master bedroom opens
to a balcony that provides views of
the inlet, Rhode Island Sound and a
myriad of historic and architecturally
significant resort homes.

OPPOSITE Seabright was designed
for gracious living and indoor spaces
form a seamless connection with
outdoor spaces.

ABOVE A seemingly weightless cantilever staircase lends understated elegance to Seabright's stair tower.

ABOVE RIGHT A window seat overlooks ocean-front estates.

FAR RIGHT The formal dining room's colour palette takes its cues from the surrounding seascape.

CHAPTER 9

HIGHLAND HOUSE

Architect William Burgin turned to the Shingle Style again in 1989 to create a year-round family home situated on a sloped parcel in Jamestown, overlooking Narragansett Bay. For this home, Burgin achieves asymmetrical massing with a fanciful combination of indigenous materials and circular and angular elements. For example, the west facing elevation features a pair of intersecting cross gables. The dominant gable boasts an arched entry topped with a trio of windows arranged in a right angle, and a curved balcony positioned above a large rounded bay that opens to a wraparound porch. A pair of matchstick chimneys with stone bases and towering brick masonry bisects the other gable. A second wraparound porch balances the façade. The imaginative juxtaposition of curves and angles continues around the house. A central angular two-storey bay anchors the north facing elevation. Curved brackets supporting the roof overhang soften the sharp angle. A curved bracket supporting a long sloping gable with another angular bay and balcony on the east facing elevation has the same effect.

The interior spaces are designed to flow freely from formal areas to informal areas while capturing water views. And each space is also connected to the surrounding perennial gardens by way of French doors, porches and balconies.

OPPOSITE Matchstick chimneys with stone bases that graduate to brick masonry are among the distinguishing features of Highland House.

BELOW The rear elevation has a long sloping gable supported by a circular bracket and a unique angled bay with an angled balcony.

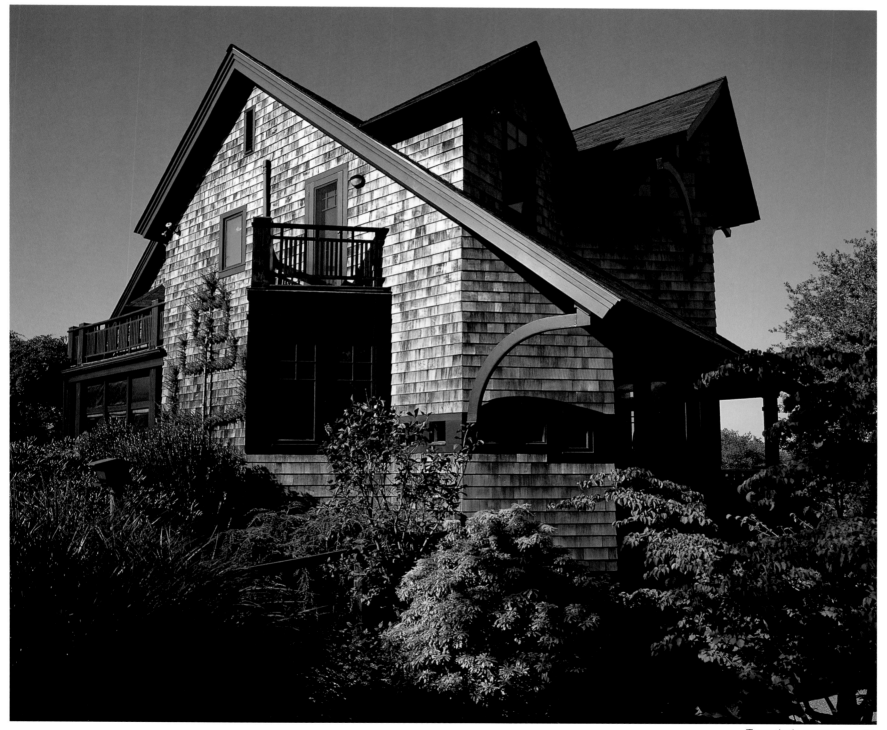

RIGHT The light-filled stairway with custom balusters is the focal point of the foyer.

BELOW The wall of windows brightens the living room and provides views of Narragansett Bay.

BELOW RIGHT Designed for entertaining, the formal dining room opens to a screened porch.

ABOVE A stone fireplace does not interrupt the continuous band of small windows.

TWENTY-FIRST CENTURY

CHAPTER 10

BLACKWATCH

Blackwatch celebrates every nuance of its natural surroundings. Sited high on a promontory in Jamestown, Rhode Island, that was once owned by Revolutionary War figure Benedict Arnold, the property affords breathtaking views of Narragansett Bay and Newport in the distance.

When considering the design for his personal weekend retreat, inspiration sprung from many sources. As design principal of the architectural firm Shope Reno Wharton, Bernard Wharton has experimented and fine-tuned his interpretations of the Shingle Style for more than three decades. As a long time admirer of Henry Hobson Richardson, he has followed his cues for developing spatial and textural innovations. And as the descendent of a prominent family who has summered in Jamestown since the 1870s, he has rambled around Shingle Style homes built for his relatives since he was a young boy – Horsehead, which can be seen from most vantage points at Blackwatch, is a landmark Shingle Style home designed in 1884 by English architect Charles Bevins for Wharton's great-uncle, John Wharton.

So without hesitation, Wharton knew that Shingle Style would enable his house to blend into the landscape and capture views from every direction.

As a result, Blackwatch resonates with historic precedent and inventiveness. Mysterious black shingles, Japanese rooflines, fieldstone chimneys, woodwork fashioned from reclaimed Douglas fir and an open, inviting layout are a testament to Shingle Style's endurance. The superior craftsmanship coupled with panoramic views celebrate the homeowners' love of the sea, as well as the creative spirit.

PREVIOUS PAGE Blackwatch.

RIGHT Blackwatch is a sophisticated composition of exaggerated peaks and swooping rooflines.

ABOVE Blackwatch's dark palette lets the house recede into the landscape, especially when viewed from passing boats.

RIGHT Early Shingle Style's Japanese influences came into play at the front entry.

ABOVE The dining room
comprises half of the great
room. Douglas fir timbers
were sourced from the
same New England bogs
that produced the knees for
the USS *Constitution*.

LEFT A granite fireplace
with curved ship's knee
braces is the focal point
of the living room.

CHAPTER 11

OUT TO SEA

On August 29, 1778 the Continental Army fought British forces in the Battle of Rhode Island. The pivotal event in Revolutionary War history took place near the northern tip of Aquidneck Island in Portsmouth, Rhode Island. Centuries later, the terrain near the battlefield has remained virtually unchanged with time tumbled stone walls, fields, streams and stretches of sandy beach along Narragansett Bay.

When architects John Grosvenor and Paul Weber of Newport Collaborative Architects, Inc. were commissioned to design one of the first homes in an upscale enclave associated with the exclusive Carnegie Abbey Club and Resort in Portsmouth, they instinctively chose Shingle Style. The vernacular not only celebrates Rhode Island's rich architectural heritage, but allowed the architects to design a home with an open floor plan that maximized sweeping views of the bay. Since Out to Sea was built in 2004, some of the regions leading architects have followed suit and designed extraordinary examples of Shingle Style in the same neighbourhood.

Out to Sea's exterior plan boasts covered verandas, gables, bands of windows, indigenous stonework, a unique staircase tower and a mahogany front entry that mimics a nautical pilot house. A sunken mahogany roof deck hidden between the gables and roof peaks provides a stunning vantage point.

Traditional craftsmanship tailored for modern lifestyles is achieved with an open floor plan that showcases masterful Colonial-style millwork, coffered ceilings and exposed timbers. All of the living spaces are organized to flow freely from formal to informal areas. French doors opening to the first floor veranda and second storey balconies, as well as a widow's walk accessed through the third storey, provide vantage points for westerly water views, and opportunities to enjoy spectacular sunsets.

RIGHT An open air veranda leads to a north facing screened porch.

FOLLOWING PAGE Out to Sea captures the essence of Shingle Style with double gables and sweeping porch roofs.

LEFT Beautifully crafted arches custom designed by Woodmeister Corporation frame the dining room and living room.

RIGHT The veranda.

BELOW French doors connect the formal living room with the veranda and views of the bay.

CHAPTER 12
BEAVERTAIL HOUSE

Bernard Wharton, design principal of the architectural firm Shope Reno Wharton, designed Beavertail House in 2001. The impressive Shingle Style house is sited on a bluff in Jamestown, Rhode Island overlooking Narragansett Bay. Beavertail House's grand proportions are reminiscent of nineteenth-century resort homes built along New England's coast. The front elevation features a pair of gables punctuated by a dramatic staircase tower. A colonnade joins the main house to the guest house and garage. And the rear elevation repeats the classic double gable design and boasts Japanese-style veranda, pergola and screened porch strategically positioned to take advantage of panoramic views and ocean breeze.

   The interior spaces capture exquisite views and flow easily from one room to the next. There are plenty of sunny spaces for family living and gracious entertaining.

ABOVE Twin gables and a unique stair tower reminiscent of a lighthouse lend a sense of grandeur to the front elevation.

RIGHT Pairs of columns and a roof overhang with a gentle kick enhance the casual elegance of the screened porch.

ABOVE A breakfast nook occupies a bay in the kitchen resplendent with custom cabinetry.

ABOVE RIGHT The formal dining room.

FAR RIGHT The hand-painted mural and stained floors in the foyer complement the Colonial décor and the collection of New England art and antiques.

ABOVE Two separate seating areas make up the living room, while a series of French doors unify the space.

RIGHT Windows in the stair tower fill the home with an abundance of natural light.

OPPOSITE Rhode Island's changing seasons can be appreciated from a distinct vantage point in the master bedroom.

CHAPTER 13

EASTWELL HOUSE

Eastwell House presides on a parcel surrounded by acres of horse pastures, equestrian trails, vineyards, and fruit orchards that extend to the rocky shores of the Sakonnet River in Portsmouth, Rhode Island. Although the home closely resembles a century-old gentleman's farm, the Shingle Style residence was built in 2006.

Englishman and real estate developer Nick Downes collaborated with Rhode Island architect Paul Burke to design a home that blends time honored New England style with contemporary amenities, yet looks like it has always belonged to the pastoral landscape. Clad in cedar shingles with a stone foundation, the home's façade features sloping twin gables joined by a small dormer that provide the home with picturesque horizontal massing. The adjoining carriage house and garage feature an asymmetrical roofline with a gable and shed dormer.

The stone foundation and stone work framing the carriage doors emphasizes the structure's vertical massing. A veranda with a blue stone terrace encircles the main house extending outdoor living spaces and further joining the home with the rural setting.

The interior features traditional spaces such as a two-storey foyer with grand staircase, formal living room, and formal dining room, as well as thoroughly modern areas such as a gourmet kitchen, home office, exercise room, and au pair suite. Classic architectural elements such as a Double Dutch entry door, transom windows, elaborate millwork and hardwood floors imbue the home with Old World elegance.

ABOVE The brick masonry chimney pierces the veranda.
OPPOSITE A pair of columns and divided lights frames the entry.

RIGHT The circular veranda overlooks scenic farmlands.

BELOW Eastwell House evokes the look of a century-old New England farmhouse.

OPPOSITE Pairs of double-hung windows on the second storey create a sense of balance for the asymmetrical structure.

LEFT The breakfast nook is furnished with an antique New England farmhouse table and parson chairs.

BELOW The formal living room boasts custom millwork, panelling and wide-plank oak flooring. Three sets of French doors open to a bluestone terrace.

CHAPTER 14
SULTHORNE

Nestled among majestic English hornbeam, turkey oak, copper beech and tulip trees, many would assume that Sulthorne was constructed in the same era as the venerable neighbouring estates that include Richard Morris Hunt's Ochre Court and The Breakers, Peabody and Stearns' Vinland, and Henry Hobson Richardson's William Watts Sherman House. However, this elegant Shingle Style home was built in 2005. Paul Weber, the homeowner and an architect at Newport Collaborative Architects, Inc. has designed numerous

Shingle Style residences for clients throughout New England. Interestingly enough, his great-grandfather, Alex Donaldson, and his grandfather, John Donaldson, experimented with the Shingle Style during the nineteenth century while working at the architectural firm of Donaldson and Meier in Michigan. Their Shingle Style Belle Isle Park project in Michigan was featured in an 1887 issue of the *American Architect and Building News* and Vincent Scully's *The Architecture of the American Summer: The Flowering of the Shingle Style* published in 1989.

So choosing Shingle Style for his own home was a natural extension of Weber's personal architectural heritage and his design portfolio.

Shingle Style well suits the historic context of the legendary Ochre Point neighbourhood, as well as his young family's active lifestyle. Sited where the Florence Lyman Gilded Age estate once presided until it was razed in the 1950s, the property still retains the original nineteenth-century Shingle Style barn that serves as a vestige to the past. The new home was thoughtfully positioned near the original home site to preserve the landscape architecture and take advantage of morning light. During excavation, relics such as eighteenth-century Delft tiles, glass fragments and bricks were unearthed and now adorn the home as unique conversation pieces.

Weber's design skillfully blends classic Shingle Style elements such as sweeping gables, a porte-cochere, covered verandas, staircase tower and a whimsical stone chimney that pierces a gable with a modern open and airy floor plan.

BELOW LEFT Multi-paned windows in the formal living room provide views of rare nineteenth-century specimen trees and a neighbouring estate.

BELOW RIGHT The fireplace in the formal living room features vintage Pewbic Pottery tiles. The Arts and Crafts pottery is prized for its unique iridescent glazes.

RIGHT The main staircase with a continuous banister becomes a sculptural element as it serves as a backdrop in the formal dining room.

ABOVE The modern kitchen features traditional white custom cabinetry and a backsplash fashioned from vintage Pewbic Pottery tiles. The architect salvaged the art pottery as a young boy from a house that was being torn down near his childhood home in Michigan.

LEFT Beaded board ceiling, shingled posts and a slate floor lend elegance to the covered porch.

ABOVE A custom headboard fashioned from mahogany and a vintage cotton sail reflects the homeowners' passion for sailing.

RIGHT From concept to completion, a model and renderings show the evolution of the home's design.

CHAPTER 15

BANCROFT ON THE BLUFFS

LEFT A new front entry dropoff centres on a restored front stair with an Oriental-inspired roofline.

RIGHT Pudding stones, a conglomerate rock mixture of sand, pebbles and quartz, are an integral part of the landscape architecture.

When artist John Chandler Bancroft returned from a pilgrimage to Japan in 1895 he employed noted architect William Ralph Emerson to design a Shingle Style mansion on a cliff in Middletown overlooking Sachuest Point and the Atlantic Ocean. Emerson, a distant cousin of Ralph Waldo Emerson, was a Boston-based architect and an early pioneer of the Shingle Style. He designed many significant Shingle Style resort homes along the rugged coastlines of Maine and Boston's North Shore. Although Emerson designed several homes in Newport including the Sanford Covell Villa, Bancroft's house represents one of his only surviving Shingle Style designs in Newport.

Bancroft greatly admired Oriental art and was an avid collector of Japanese prints amassing more than three thousand artworks. Emerson incorporated many Japanese features, such as pagoda-style rooflines and woodwork with Asian motifs. Frederick Law Olmsted, Jr. was also commissioned to design a Chinese garden.

Sadly, during the mid-twentieth century, the building changed owners and was divided into apartments. Eventually Bancroft's estate fell into a state of disrepair and was sold to a real estate developer at auction in 2005. The following year, architect John Grosvenor and his team from Newport Collaborative Architects, Inc. were enlisted to fashion an adaptive reuse of the historic Shingle Style home. The architects reconfigured the building to accommodate eleven luxury condominium residences. Along the way they added a wing with a series of complementary porches and gables to create a seamless connection between nineteenth-century designs and twenty-first-century rehabilitation. All of the residences boast ocean views and modern amenities.

LEFT Although the façade has complex geometries, the overall design successfully exhibits classic Shingle Style.

BELOW The two-storey addition to an existing octagonal tower provides panoramic views of the Atlantic Ocean.

BIBLIOGRAPHY

Downing, Antoinette F., and Vincent J. Scully, Jr. *The Architectural Heritage of Newport, Rhode Island*. Second Edition. (New York: Clarkeson N. Potter, 1967)

Lewis, Arnold. *American Country Houses of the Gilded Age (Sheldon's 'Artistic Country-seats')*. (New York: Dover Publications, 1982)

Roth, Leland M. *McKim, Mead & White Architects*. (New York: Harper and Row, 1983)

Scully, Vincent. *The Architecture of the American Summer: The Flowering of the Shingle Style*. (New York: Rizzoli, 1989)

Scully, Vincent. *The Shingle Style*. (New Haven: Yale University Press, 1955)

Scully, Vincent. *The Shingle Style Today or the Historian's Revenge*. (New York: Braziller, 1974)

Scully, Vincent. *The Shingle Style: Architectural Theory and Design from Richardson to the Origins of Wright*. (New Haven: Yale University Press, 1955)

White, Samuel G. *The Houses of McKim, Mead & White*. (New York: Rizzoli, 1997)

Wilson, Richard Guy. *McKim, Mead & White Architects*. (New York: Rizzoli, 1983)

INDEX

Page entries in *italics* refer to captions and illustrations

American Architect and Building News 31, 100
American Colonial style 7, 10, 21, *33*, 40, *43*, 45, 49, 53, 56, 82, *90*
The Architectural Heritage of Newport, Rhode Island 6
The Architecture of the American Summer: The Flowering of the Shingle Style 100
Arts and Crafts 6, *26*, *33*, *102*

Bancroft on the Bluffs 106, *106–109*
Beavertail House 88, *88–93*
Bell, Isaac, House 6, 7, 8, *42–7*, 43, 64, *64*
Berkeley, Bishop George 21, *21*
Bevins, Charles 7, 49, *49*, *53*, 76
Bigelow, William 21
Blackwatch 76, *76–81*
Breakers, The 6, 100
Burgin, William 8, 64, 70
Burke, Paul 8, 9

Castle Hill Lighthouse *11*
Chalet Stables *24–7*, 25
Channel Bells *48–53*, 49

Downes, Nick 94
Downing, Antoinette 6

Eastwell House 94, *94–9*
Emerson, William Ralph 106

Gill, Irving 6, 56
Greene & Greene 6
Griswold, John N.A. 25
Grosvenor, John 8, 25, 82, *82*, 106

Highland House *55*, *70–73*
Hunt, Richard Morris 25, 100

Japan, Japanese style 7, 36, *60*, 76, *76*, 88, 106

King, Edward, Villa 6

Luce, Clarence 7

McKenzie House 56
McKim, Mead & White 6, 7, 21, 36, 43, *44*, 49, 64
Marble House *17*

Newport Casino 6, 8, *14*, 43
New York Sketchbook of Architecture 21, 31

Olde English 7, 31
Olmsted, Frederick Law, Jr. 56, *60*, 106
Out to Sea 82, *82–7*

Peabody and Stearns 49, 100
Perry, Commodore M. 7
Pewbic Pottery *102*, *103*
Price, Bruce 7
Preservation Society of Newport County 45

Queen Anne 6, 7, 10, 28, 31, 49

Richardson, H.H. 7, 31, 76, 100
Rosecliff 6

Seabright 64, *64–9*
Scully, Vincent 6, 8, 11, 25, 100
Sherman, William Watts, House 6, 7, *29–33*, 100

The Shingle Style: Architectural Theory and Design from Richardson to the Origins of Wright 6
The Shingle Style Today, or the Historian's Revenge 8
Stick Style 10, 22, 25, *25*
Sulthorne 100, *100–105*

Tilton, Samuel, House 6, 36, *36–41*

Upjohn, Richard 6

Weber, Paul 8, 82, *82*, 100–101
Wharton, Bernard 8, 76, 88
Wildeacre *5*, 56, *56–63*, 64
Whitehall *19–21*

ACKNOWLEDGEMENTS

The photography and text came to fruition by the extraordinary enthusiasm, generosity and hospitality bestowed on us by the architects, homeowners and stewards of the structures portrayed in this book. Many thanks to the following individuals and organizations: Bernard Wharton, Jennifer Walsh, John and Mary Ellen Grosvenor, Bill and Dinny Burgin, Paul and Bonnie Weber, Gary and Gail Bay, Dorrance Hamilton, Sandra Craig, Betsy Gooding, Nick Downes, Jim Roiter, James Buttrick, Woodmeister Corporation, the Whitehall Committee of the National Society of the Colonial Dames of America in the State of Rhode Island and Providence Plantations, Salve Regina University, International Tennis Hall of Fame, and the Preservation Society of Newport County. And special thanks to our dear friend and mentor, Richard Guy Wilson.

FEATURED ARCHITECTS
William L. Burgin, AIA
Burgin Lambert Architects
150 Bellevue Avenue
Newport, RI 02840
www.williamburgin.com

Paul Burke Architects, AIA
311 Vacluse Avenue
Middletown, RI 02842
www.paulburkearchitects.com

John K. Grosvenor, AIA
Principal
Newport Collaborative Architects, Inc.
38 Washington Square
Newport, RI 02840
www.ncarchitects.com

Paul Weber, AIA
Senior Associate
Newport Collaborative Architects, Inc.
38 Washington Square
Newport, RI 02840
www.ncarchitects.com

Bernard Wharton
Founding Partner
Shope Reno Wharton
18 Marshall Street, Suite 114
South Norwalk, CT 06854
www.shoperenowharton.com

CONTRIBUTORS

ABOUT THE AUTHOR

Cheryl Hackett first became intrigued by architecture and interior design when she lived in Helsinki, Finland as an American Field Service exchange student in 1982. The first time the teenager toured Eliel Saarinen's summer home with her Finnish host family, Hvittrask's inventive blend of shingles, logs, stones and spatial wonders enchanted her and left an indelible mark on her life.

The following year, Cheryl became smitten with Shingle Style architecture when she had the opportunity to live in the historic William Watts Sherman House while enrolled at Salve Regina University in Newport, Rhode Island. She often retreated to a quiet corner of the library designed by Stanford White to pore over literature and journalism textbooks. The room's graceful proportions, intricately carved paneling and gilding often distracted her from her studies, yet deepened her appreciation for highly original architecture and interior design.

After earning a bachelor's and master's degree, Cheryl has worked as a freelance editor, writer and stylist for nearly two decades. Her articles about architecture, historic preservation, interior design and lifestyles have appeared in many national magazines including *La Vie Claire*, *Victorian Homes*, *Romantic Homes*, *Classic American Homes*, *Coastal Living*, *Cottage Style*, *Romantic Living*, *Country Decorating Ideas*, *Kids Rooms*, *Kitchens*, *Cape Cod & Islands Home* and *Yankee*.

During her career, Cheryl has had the opportunity to produce magazine articles about many nineteenth-century Shingle Style houses including the William Watts Sherman House, Isaac Bell House, Tilton House and C.H. Baldwin House for *Victorian Homes*. She's also published articles about twentieth- and twenty-first-century Shingle Style homes in Rhode Island and Nantucket for *Romantic Homes*.

Cheryl returned to Salve Regina University in 2000 as an adjunct professor and has taught many writing classes. She was selected to speak at the thirteenth Annual Cultural and Historic Preservation Conference at Salve Regina University in 2009, and the American Literature Association's national conferences held in Cambridge, Massachusetts in 2001 and 2003. Her topics focused on Gilded Age architecture and interior design.

ABOUT THE PHOTOGRAPHER

Motivated by the magic of light and expression, Kindra Clineff has been working as a professional photographer for the past eighteen years and specializes in architectural, lifestyle, and travel photography. Born in the Midwest, her family migrated to the Connecticut River Valley, desiring the colonial simplicity New England offered. She is now based in Topsfield, Massachusetts, and her work encompasses the globe as she shoots collateral and editorial assignments for a variety of national publications including *La Vie Claire*, *Coastal Living*, *Victorian Homes*, *Romantic Homes* and *Yankee*, as well as corporate, advertising and academic accounts. She is an avid gardener and beekeeper and when not chasing light, she can be found cultivating heirloom vegetables and taming the perennial garden at her seventeenth-century home.

ABOUT RICHARD GUY WILSON

Richard Guy Wilson holds the Commonwealth Professor's Chair in Architecture at the University of Virginia, where he is also Chair of the Department of Architectural History. A frequent lecturer for universities, museums and professional groups, Wilson has also published widely and was the Thomas Jefferson Visiting Fellow at Downing College, Cambridge, United Kingdom. He has served as an advisor and commentator for a number of television programmes and has been the curator and author for major museum exhibitions. Wilson has received a number of academic honors; among them a Guggenheim fellow, prizes for distinguished writing, and in 1986 he was made an honorary member of the American Institute of Architects.

Frances Lincoln Limited
4 Torriano Mews
Torriano Avenue
London NW5 2RZ
www.franceslincoln.com

Newport Shingle Style

First Frances Lincoln edition 2010

A catalogue record for this book is available from the British Library.

978-0-7112-2937-2

Printed and bound in China

1 2 3 4 5 6 7 8 9

PAGES 1 & 2 Isaac Bell House.
PAGES 4–5 Wildacre.